Family
Feelings of
Little Tanie

Family Feelings of Little Tanie

Breaking the Illusions Inside a Mirror

A new perspective ~ A wider horizon,

KHILY KHILACHAND

PARTRIDGE

A Penguin Random House Company

To order additional copies of this book, contact
Partridge India
000 800 10062 62
orders.india@partridgepublishing.com

www.partridgepublishing.com/india

Preface

I dedicate this edition, exclusively to my grandmother, Prof. Rekha Prasad "Curly Yashman" and to all grandmothers as herself.

This book is a gift to families blessed with old ladies, known as grannies.

It's got 12 poems, 12 letters, 12 jokes and 12 stories.

Through this book, I wish to convey, that every grandmother is special, and so is the relationship which they share with their grand children. Therefore, we must cherish this beautiful bond.

Introductory Poem

Rex Rox

(I mean Rekha Rocks)
The heights you've reached,
are hard to retain
The goals you've achieved,
are hard to attain
Ever dearest granny;
my victory, my stride..
..I find you there,
Wherever I hide
I may end up with my stock,
but you completely rock

More about me

To understand my third and final edition, which is, this very book; one has to go through my debut volume followed by the second one; Creations of Little Tanie and More Creations of Little Tanie, respectively.

Also, my favourite movies, Barbie and The Diamond Castle and The Barbie Diaries have to be watched, to be able to understand me better; as this would hint a picture of my personality reflected in my write ups.

I love the songs from both of my favourite movies. They inspired me to write. The movies are a "must watch" I'd advise; and the songs.. a "must hear".. lovely lyrics and music for folks with traditional-ish kinda taste.

I suggest my readers to have fondness for Barbie dolls as myself. I simply love them and collect them like crazy.

My home's full of many of them. Therefore I also dedicate my books to Barbies.

Another movie that I admire, is Now and Then and thus this book is also a dedication to Girly and Womanly Friendship, represented in all the three movies which I love: Barbie in a Diamond Castle, The Barbie Diaries and Now and Then.

I believe that language is a reflection of mind and mind is a reflection of reality. Thus, one must speak and write well enough, to project self.

We portray our image with the way we present ourselves, in terms of our speech and text.

Poems

Poem no. 1

Tanny with Granny

Together we spend..
..the moments so memorable
Together we tie..
..the knot of affection !!
Tanny and Granny..
..a duo worth attention
The twosome so awesome,
that no one could beat
Sometimes we've quarrelled,
And always hoped not to repeat
Tanny with Granny
..a picture ..complete!

Poem no. 2

**To my granny,
I devote my life**

When I see you..
..I see eternity
When I look at you,
I feel God speak to me
You are my luck,
you are my charm
In your arms,
lay my eternity

Poem no. 3

Troubling my granna ..is fun!

Oh! Granna
.. don't mind
You know..
..it's fun
I know, you think
that it's just not done
But it's such a mischief
Mischievous Merry..
..behind me when you run
And when I defeat you
in an argument..
..it's such a battle won!!

Poem no. 4

Grand mom, my first love

Whenever I begin to
bond with someone,
I try to find your reflection
in that person
The bond we share..
..so cute, so magical
It's like an entire tale undone
..like a whole story begun!!

Poem no. 5

Rex, Curly, Granz

You rock my world,
you raise me high
I comfort you, whenever I try
I can assure you, that
you'd be missing me
..wherever you'd be
Oh! Granz,
at times, you don't understand me
Would you ever realise,
what you mean to me?

Poem no. 6

**You're Special!
.. most special!!**

No matter how much I have
differences with you..,
at the end of the day,
I come to you submissively
This is the reason, a whole
volume of poems..
..to you I dedicate, exclusively
For you've got to know
You ought to know..
..the gem and jewel you mean to me

Poem no. 7

Tough Grans

Sometimes a soft sunshine
The other times, a cool
and soothing shade
This is how my granna is
I wonder how'd she be
after a decade
She's tough and thick
skinned when needed
and hard to persuade

Poem no. 8

Granna, my bundle of joy

Granna, my thunder, my wonder
Granna, often falls into blunder
Granna.. sometimes, acts as an envoy
Granna.. my thorough bundle of joy
Being with granna..
..I whole heartedly enjoy

Poem no. 9

She brings out the best in me

My grandmother,
whom I owe a lot
My grandmother,
who has raised me
from the time I was a tiny tot
She is the reason, I want
to be an achiever
She is the source.. ..that
I dare to dream
She pulls me,
like a hurt knee
She brings out..
..the best in me

Poem no. 10

My idol.. my granny

She's been my hero,
she's brought me up with all her care
To leave her mid way, I'd never dare
She'd always be in all my wishes
She'd rest forever in my prayer
It is unexplainable..
..the bondage we share

Poem no. 11

My cutie pie

Sweet in all her gestures,
Sweet in every way
She's my sweetheart,
that's what I always say
Together we learn..
..the manner in which life carries on
Together we enjoy and play

Poem no. 12

You.. I aspire, my grans

You.. upon whom I swear, my grans
You.. my top most gear, my grans
Between us.. is a beautiful relationship,
dear granny
You're the one I admire, my grans
I admire you the most, dear granny
You.. I aspire, my grans
I aspire you with boast, dear granny

Letters to my Grandma

..Curly Prasad

Letter no. 1

Dear Granny,
Hope you to be going great guns.
You must take care of your health.
I wish you long life, always.
You must know that you're the
one I look upon, look up to and
idealise...... Without you, I wouldn't
have existed, I realise.
Love you granny
Miss you
Take care
Yours always,
Tanny

Letter no. 2

Grandmother, my ever dearest..
How've you been? I hope and pray,
that you're all fine. I'm doing alright
by God's grace and your prayers.
Grandmother, I must tell you,
that you're the one.. ..who always
stands up by me. You're the one..
..who cares. In your divine presence..
..my spirituality flares.
I think to myself.. ..when shall
I be capable enough to reward
you for all that you've offered.
One day soon.. ..grandmother,
I should be able to return to you,
more than what you
showered me with.
With warm wishes
Yours ever,
Tanmeyta

Letter no. 3

Naani,
How's life?
I guess everything all set.

Naani, I'm ever glad.. ..that I'm
blessed with a grandmother as you.
You're actually one among few.
I bet you've been worrying bout
me. That's pretty usual of you.
Don't forget to take your
medicines at time.

Lately, I've been fixed with some issues.
Seeking your advice
Truly yours,
Tanmeyta Yashman

Letter no. 4

Grandma, my love
Guess what?
Once again.. ..it's time to rejoice. Coz
I'm coming to you in a short while. In
no time, your princess will be right
in front of your eyes. With your
picture in mind, every morning I rise.
You're gonna get the forbidden goodies;
but for that.. ..condition applies; *wink*.
All your nice outfits wait for me; I
wonder when I'll grow their size.
Oh! Grandma..
..you're such a blessing in disguise

Forever yours,
Your ever loving
Little Tanie

Letter no. 5

Dearest Grand mum,
May my letter see you in all
your best. I expect you to be
taking good care of yourself.
Been missing you as usual. You
must know that you're a jewel.
You're my energy, you're my fuel.
Heard bout your upcoming
agendas. Do your best, grans!
Ever yearning to hug you tight..
yours,
T D Y

Letter no. 6

Sup gran
Mah sweety-poo,
mah honeykins
Been upto mischief? I gotta
raise mah brow then!
You gotta be kiddin' around.. ..your
usual stuff, I know!
N E neu plans, mah granny grans ??
Waitin' fu reply
Ciao sweetykins
Luv,
Tan

Letter no. 7

Sweetest love,
How's my baby doing?
Having chocolates? Naughty naughty!
wink. Well, you could have them,
provided they're sugarfree *lol* !

Take meals in time, sweets

No worry bout nothin'

Do as you like, leave the rest to God!
Take a chill pill
Miss you babe
Muah
Always,
Tanie

Letter no. 8

My dear dear dearrrrr Granny,
Hope things are cool there.
Everythin' rockin' here too granna.
My love, you need to expose
more.. ..expose your day-
to-day details, to me.
I wish my mail brings you grace, am
ever hungry for your embrace.
Eagerly waitin' to see you
Yours forever,
Tanmeya

Letter no. 9

Hi Gran mum,
How's life treatin' ya? All well, I expect.
Am all good here.
Missing the little ways you
enlighten my world..
..a small world.
Been dyin' to hear from ya.
Stop being lazy; get going...
Ready, steady, on your
marks, get set, go.......!!!!
Write to me
Catch ya soon
Yours always,
Meya

Letter no. 10

Ever dearest granny,
It's been long since we talked. I really
hope everything to be all fine with you.
I can't wait to hold you.., hug
you.., feel you.. ..from within.
Until we catch up again,
keep fingers crossed.
With warm wishes and affections
Your loving grand daughter,
Tanmeyta Darshee Yashman
P. S. – I like to tease you, my girlfriend

Letter no. 11

Hey Grans
Long time, no sees !
What's keepin' you from writin' to me ?
Busy, busy, busy.. huh ?
Do remember..
I miss you a lot
Am your ever darling grand daught

Smiling,
Tanz

Letter no. 12

My darling grand mom,
Wad yu been up to? Watz
neu at yur end?
When we meet d next, do tell
me.. ..how much d'yu miss me!!??
Been quite some time we met, daht's
a challenge, pon which I can bet !
Desperately waitin' to see yu
Yur sunshine,
Darshee

Granny Jokes

Joke no. 1

Dun' worry bou d bans
Jus do yur ting, grans
Cuz men switches to mans
Precious packages've begun
to come in vans
Gypsies move in caravans
Dis fontz comic sans

Joke no. 2

Dun grill
Take a chill pill
Ultimately I'm yur 'will'
So, yu gotta show, yu're nill
Yu're empty, unless I fill

Joke no. 3

Go wacky like granny
with granny glasses
latest trend,
Granny is to lend
Dependz pon d bucks yu spend
Hey, hey, hey...
nothin' to offend

Joke no. 4

Feel me say granny
Feel me speak to you
..in your 'dare' dreams
..where my mind screams

Joke no. 5

Aha! You got me there
..I got caught
You're d brainy sort
Who shuns d dumb lot
..n' am your daught
..tea pot

Joke no. 6

Come on Granny,
don' be a spoil sport!
You've got to play it well
..jus remember
your magic spell
Bravo, you can do it..
..is all I tell
What's cookin'?
There's somethin' fishy
I smell

Joke no. 7

You gotta get your _ movin'
Jive it up
Shake it
You gotta get grovin'
You gettin' me, grans?

Joke no. 8

Plan your parties well Naani
Do keep in mind,
the distinguished guest
..that's me, your dearest
I'm gonna rock the fest
Afterall.. I'm the best

Joke no. 9

Have you completely lost it, grans
! ?
No way !
You're not gettin' me there
Din play no pranks pon you, sweetykins
You're gettin' me all wrong
N' am all dead
Rumours are what you spread

Joke no. 10

Indeed grannykins..
Who could beat you?
You're a potion in yourself
..a complete commotion

Joke no. 11

Yu're so naive, granny
Can't be amazed
daht yu're diabetic
...I sugar-coat yu
wid ma wordz

Joke no. 12

When you're wild,
am the most spanked child
I remember..
..when you last smiled,
your anger was all piled!!

Grandmother Stories

real "short n' crisp" ones

Story no. 1

Growing to Elegance

Once upon a time, there lived a granny
with her grand daughts, Tanny. They
both made merry together. Their
togetherhood was much talked about.
Soon Tanny grew into an elegant
lady, under her granny's guidance,
and comforted her granny
with all that she required.
Tanny and granny continued
to live happily ever after.

Story no. 2

In terms

A short while back, said a grandmother to her grand dots, "have you gone nuts, chica? You aint tell lies!". To this, grand dots replied, "with your gentle care and affection, I've become a carefree lass, grans!" And since then... grand ma and grand dots have been in terms.

Story no. 3

The First and The Last Time

There's a sweet granz. She's been such a hot babe; and her grand daughters are cool fellas. The three of them partied life, together.
One day, granz asked her lovely granddaughters, "are you two in your senses?" as they were dressed all wacky for their school 'get together'. This was the first and the last time that granz would utter such words; for she's been companying her amazing two's styles from then onwards.

Story no. 4

Technocrat

Some time ago, was a family of
four. Mama, Papa, Grandma and
a big bore. Grandma was able
to turn him into a hardcore.
Bore became a technology geek. He
invented devices that were sleek.
Thanks to grandma; credits to her...
today we enjoy gadgets that purr.

Story no. 5

Taking Charge at a Young Age

Once upon a time, long long ago, there was a girl named Meya. She lived with her grandmother, Curly. Curly was named so, because of her hair. Well, with time and age, her hair had straightened.
Meya was merely fourteen when her grand mom retired from her workplace. Meya took charge of the household at a young age. Since then, Meya stood up for grand mum, at every stage.

Story no. 6

Desperation... No Good

I know a talented artist, named
Darshika. She grows desperate for
actualisation of her art-piece.
Darshika has a concerned grand mom.
Grand mommy always explains to her,
how to have patience and be sensible.
Grand mommy tells her, "Desperation
is no good, dear". Darshika has tried to
imbibe on her grand mommy's advice.
Darshika and grand mommy
make a perfect twosome.

Story no. 7

Practice... Without a Fail

Long long back, a grandmother always taught her much cared about grandchildren that must devote themselves to whichever skill they wish to adopt. It is important to build a liking for the thing we wish to do: only then can we dedicate to our work, our objective, task... goal. The only way to perfection, is practice. So, granny said, 'it is necessary that we keep on practicing; practice without a fail and continue trying to give our best'. The children did as their grandmother advised and thus they were able to become successful professionals in their life.

Story no. 8

Attendance ~ without a miss

Granny says, classes and sessions are never to be skipped. One must try, not to miss a class! She said, only in rare cases one might think of not going for a session. Children understood what granny meant. She must have meant that if one is hindered by health, weather or family reasons, then that person could give it a thought, as to not attending a skilled slot. Those who are able to give 100% attendance, can hit there..where few people can.

Story no. 9

Mutual Admiration

A few decades ago, a family of four spent a content living. The family had a grandmum, her son and daughter in law, and their daughter. All of them had liking and respect for each other. They honoured one another in every regard, in all sense. This is what grandmum had made each family learn, afterall..... that there is peace and harmony in relationships or families and work places for that matter, where people have mutual admiration. They must show regard, be it anyone.

Story no. 10

Focus

Determination is the key to victory, told a grandmother to her grandsons. Grandsons, Abby and Addy, were very naughty by nature. Their behaviour being hyper active, they had a fugitive attitude and thus got easily distracted while whatever they did. Gradually, grandmother Mrs. Amy Ry was able to teach them, the way to focus on their goals. She taught them the necessity to have clear aims and ambitions and to be able to achieve them in order to make friends and family proud.

Story no. 11

Viewing our world with diverse perspective

Grandmama Ananya was very fond of her granddaughter Aanya. She was her favourite among five of her grandchildren. Aanya being the youngest of them all. Also, because Aanya was the most obedient amongst her other cousins and siblings. Grandmama told Aanya, that there can be various ways in which we could see the same thing. She said, one must have a versatile outlook for various objects; the perspective being wide and varied.

Grandmama told all her loved grandchildren, that they must have an expanded horizon. She had a message for us all. "Expand your horizon!"

Story no. 12

Unfavourable Conditions

Once upon a time, there lived a Yashman family, they were very affectionate and committed towards each other. The head of the family was the Grandmother. She was a lady of substance and took good care of her family. She nurtured her family with her loving care and concern. Grandmother explained to all her children, that to be successful, one has to learn to give his / her best..even in cramped situations. She further suggested to all her children, to be tough from within, in order to be an achiever. A true winner is the one, who can fulfil tasks even in unfavourable conditions.

Tanie's Thoughts and Rhymes

Screaming ~ Deep Thoughts and Flaring ~ Steep Rhymes

Whatever happens, our hometown
would remain a loved place.. as it feels
that our forefathers built it for us.

We are the same species
if you get what I say.

How I wish we shared a kin,
toasting upon the eternity..
May my wish come alive..
So feel my message dance,
sing and rhyme to you~
~the warmth and depth it holds..
..every statement thus it says,
is a mystical tale it unfolds !!

One must not choose words
of hatred and enmity..

as its impact is equal to the one who
listens to it and the one who says it
All it gives is.. ..grief !
Dream to be beautiful..
..in words, speech, voice and behaviour
..And appearance? Well,
sometimes... at least.

The past is only for realising.
Storms of emotions are good between
close people, for they are an indication
of normal course of environment.
After every storm, comes
a peaceful breeze..
The past is only for realising !!

Those who love to express
in words, love to write..
..They forget whether it's day or night.
Once they begin, they just
keep flowing (like I do)
Everything else is forgotten,
in this flow.

Touching statement from
a separated friend..

"I didn't walk away from you.....
You didn't care enough to stop me"

Prayer
We pray
Dear God
Come to us
And strengthen our thoughts
Stay with us, within us
And provide us with peace..
Thank you for all your mornings
Keep us playing
Amen

Focus>> Determination>>
>>Aims>> Goals>> Objectives>>
>>Aspirations>> Ambitions
Moving towards aims and ambitions,
our thoughts must be pure and
so must be our intensions

Prayer
Forgive me for my sins, as I
realise and regret them
I have been confronting the Tests

and apologetic with guilt, for
every mistake that I've made
Amen

Few roads lead to victory
Some paths go where success resides
Yet all the ways must guide us towards..
..Self Realisation and Salvation !!

Writer is a guardian
And one's writing is one's ward
They rest in books.. like
mother and child

I'm a rhymes player
My games all fair
I believe in being a mayor
May God and Goodness
answer my prayer

On a day that brings pressures,
is a chapter that brings treasures..
which makes us realise simple pleasures

Some things come to an
over for starting again

One births the other
..as in the following »
HappinesS>Sorrows
SorrowS>Smiles
SmileS>Sadness
SadnesS>Sympathy
SympathY>You
YoU>Us
US>Strength
StrengtH>Happiness
And back to..
HappinesS>Sorrows
Where one ends.. another begins !!
A cycle that continues forever !!!

Punishment Prayer
If ever your loved ones cry,
pray upon the cosmos
and the creator who creates us all..
..that a cosmic storm hits them
all who become the reason for
your loved ones' precious tears

Be facetious all your life
But don't regret what you've been
No Regrets

Smart people don't regret
They improve
Be smart, not douche *wink*

Keep your goodness intact
Don't lose it
While discard the illness that
find a way inside you
Know your goodness
(love, humanity, innocence,
faith, aspirations etc.)
Also know your illness
(Dragging, Lethargy, Distrust,
Foolishness etc.)
Give yourself "best of luck"
while commencing and new subject.

One of the best characteristics
we can possess are
Analytical Expression..
Verbal Expression..
the skill to speak and write
(a natural skill worth retaining)

No one or perhaps nothing in this world
is absolutely good or absolutely bad

Everything and everyone possesses
some or the other good as well
as bad characteristics
Large family living under a roof..
living in peace, unity and love..
..is a world nearly perfect
One must celebrate a
nearly perfect world.

Peace, harmony and love must
be one's soul and religion
One must speak spirituality, not fence
A fence that offenses
A boundary so rude
..the fence of idol worshiping religion
Spirituality is a garden
Boundary wall to this garden is
utter rudeness to mankind
A garden is best without a fence
No fencing
No boundaries
But trees at guard
Huge and bulky trees
Trees of wisdom
Trees of purity
Trees of sanity

Trees of compassion
Trees acting as a barrier for
evils to get inside the garden
Impure beings must be
stopped from entering
"the fragile garden" and
ruining its merry life

Life is at its best, when made
simple and not complicated
Life is at its best when
prevented from danger..
..danger of wounds

All fate.. all destiny
Some who didn't deserve to live..
..have a beautiful "today"
Some who had a glorious "past"
and were beautiful within..
..have an ugly "present"
All fate,. All destiny
Not fair at times
May kind Lord do justice
Amen

God comes in form of will, a strong will

New hopes
New horizons
But same feelings
Same emotions
Desire to stay united with one's family
A family that must include God
God.. a will, a strong will

The ones who feed trash, desire to
see the better race at losing end
Some people feed garbage to those who
can be better than they themselves
This is the reality of "Jealousy"
A hard reality
The story of "Envy"

Motive behind a neutral behaviour ~
1. Peaceful Life
2. No unnecessary interaction
3. No mess, no muddle, no meddle
4. No fuss, no hassle, no strife.......
5. Just oneself and one's God..........!!
God ~ A Divine Power, A
Sacred Energy !

New hopes, new beginnings..

Every day brings a new light
New hopes, new beginnings, new start
Every violent storm from "yesterday"
turns into a soothing breeze "today"
A breeze that brings....
New hopes, new beginnings, new start
But the bitter reality remains..
Nothing is for ever
Nothing is permanent except change

Gratefulness must we express for
the purity brought by the sunrise
time and the positivity it spreads
Reviving our soul each day and
rejuvenating our spirits

All that we have today
All that we've got
We must respect them
all and thank God
..because life offers comfort now
It may not always
Thus, we must cherish
each gift we receive
We must relish each treasure we get

When a Goddess smiles,
a mother smiles
An epic is created in a deal that's brisk
A star is born in the cradle of risk
A mind is innovative when
the spirit is frisk
On a stormy day, in the cradle of risk..
a star takes birth when a
Goddess smiles at disk

Only for God, today I write
Only for God, today I give in
I be more sensible, just for God
I feel more lively, just because of God
It's God everywhere
It's God all around
I <3 God
Because of God, life is merry
God is everything I seek !
May I see God in all my dreams..
I make a loving wish !

Begin Your Day With A Positive Poem

With our will and vigour
a position we secure

The atmosphere refreshing
its essence so pure

The morning calls
it feels so sure
that it guarantees
every weary has a cure

Sensibility pokes
a mind that's mature

Good Morning !

Tanie, a singing dream

I ran after it; saw it unfold
Chased it like crazy and
named it Tanie
Tanie, my name
Tanie, a person never the same
Tanie, a mischief, a fame
..sometimes a feeble little flame
A dream I kept running after
A dream that made me chase itself
I knew that it was a mirage
..and I let it play me like an elf

Clear Intensions

The clarity of words, ever so evident
Mind conveyed with
intensions so eminent
Leaving a mark; leaving a scar
Effective as trigger; impactful
as tears' shower
Flickering as flame; twinkling as star
Feeble as a shimmering light
Smooth as a flow of insight
Gentle as breeze
Strong as a droplet to freeze

Flower

It affects unconditionally
And decorates life beautifully
.. a flower, brings pleasure..
conventionally
.. a flower, a mode of passion
that evokes emotions traditionally
Innocent and appealing;
distributes love
The symbol of daintiness..
a delicate flower
and yet a hint of strength;
an indication of power

Light

Light.. turns surrounding bright
Light.. often makes
environment 'just right'
Light.. sometimes invokes
thoughts to take a flight
Light.. towards a ray of
hope, what one might

Book

It supports as a friend;
it acts as a guide
It makes insight grow bigger,
it turns horizons wide
It's always faithful, once allied
It stays with and for,
till one has died
Its morals are used, in
life they are applied
A book.. by which we must abide

Dreams

Dreams may break; or
they may come true
Their prominence reflects,
in the way they bru
Dreams may scare; or they
may make one scream
Evident in our lives,
flowing like a stream

Truth

Truth.. to be spoken always,
yet hard to sustain
Truth.. sometimes a reason
behind our suffering and pain
Truth.. a thin dividing line
between brawn and brain

Life

What is life?
It's a struggle
It makes one quarry; it
makes one juggle
A conquest forever; an answer
to overcome trouble
Life is nothing but a butterfly
that makes us chase itself
Life is everything that is
needed to build oneself

Colours

They add vibrancy to life,
They bring up potency
They speak for their efficiency
They define various moods
They tell if a person broods
Colours.. a form of expression
Colours.. a medium of impression

Angels

Silently they come and
enlighten our minds
In difficulties they help, or solve
a problem when one finds
A source of guidance.. ..leading
us to betterment
..they show us the path
to enhancement

Gifts

They're a symbol of affection
They draw the seekers' attention
Often mistaken for bribe;
it is how one might embibe
Gifts.. a token of love and joy
Gifts.. have always spoken of employ

Moods

They swing.., to hasty
conclusions they bring
Delicate is its string
Sometimes joyful, the
other times boring
Moods.. often calm; seldom roaring

A Road Less Walked Upon

The door to a bright future,
opens less often
Opportunity knocks rarely
The pathway to dreamland
is hardly ever explored
The route to success being
even more self imposed

Passion

An aura within;
a halo of sentiments
Once ignited, speaks for itself
Passion.. it is what one implements

Peace

It is what one shares
To break it, one dares
Peace.. a fairy who relieves
Peace.. an achievement in
which one believes
Peace.. takes away grieves

Love

A blanket of comfort,
so cosy and soothing
It makes us realise our existence
It makes us feel alive and breathing
Love.. a garden of emotion
Love.. a magic potion

Childhood

A time of utter bliss
A time of innocence;
A time.. free from worries,
A time.. free from crisis
Childhood.. the most
cherished part of lifetime
Childhood.. finds no reason for crime

Emotions

At times, gurgling like flood
The other times withdrawing,
like drought
We're made up of it
It flows in our blood
Love and hatred open it up like a knot

Woman

She pleases with her grace
..and hugs her dear ones
into her embrace
Woman.. the source of
life, like a river
Woman.. the epitome of sacrifice,
the ultimate forgiver

Water

A colourless compound
Without which one might get astound
It offers life, with which
it's ever-bound
Enriches everyone's living
with its gurgling sound
Water.. a sheer need
Water.. sometimes a greed
Water.. always a feed

Fire

Flaring with anger,
burning with heat
Flares and glares and
stares with no repeat
Burns without discrimination
Knows no criteria of elimination
Fire.. a screaming blend
Fire.. sometimes a forbidden trend

Creativity

It comes spontaneously and
impresses instantly
It speaks its tale
and uncovers a veil
Creativity.. explores paths
that are less thought about
Creativity.. speaks of itself
silently, without a doubt

Gems and Jewels

Enchanting with its glitz and glitter
Yet sometimes they could
be extremely bitter
Often mesmerising, and still deceiving
A symbol of power, that's
what gems and jewels are

Family

We cannot do without the
clutches of which,
a family is that pitch
Why not forget all ills from past
A family is thus meant
to have a blast

Destiny

Destiny is something which
no one can fight
It stores fate and knows
what one might
It could be an evil, it can be a sprite
Destiny always knows what is right

Desires

It tries to escape, when
we try to hold it
It secures its place, when
we try to fold it
Desires are what one aspires;
to gain it, one perspires
All in all, it always inspires

A Soul Injured

A tear flowed out, without a word
Someone dear grew stout,
like a flightless bird
Something clear drew about,
when a mishap occurred
Poetess Tanmeyta shares
her creations,
like a soul injured

War

A conflict of thoughts..
..the dragging beliefs and sorts
Two great grandmothers:
Laxmi and Lalita:
the war-like lots
In their war, my image distorts

Guess and Guarantee

There are some things that
we can guess upon
There are others, upon
which we can guarantee
Whatever might be the
consequences, one can hardly
ever guarantee upon surety
Nothing is sure, for nothing is pure

Escape

Sooner or later, I'd have myself gone
In form of air.. atmosphere,
I'd be born
Then shall I see.. a bright dawn,
when from criticalities, I'd
have myself withdrawn
I visualise myself.. as a
mystical.. mythical swan
A swan escaping from troubles,
escaping being torn
Never expecting life to warn

Root and Route

The ones we recall in our wearies,
the ones whom we remember
in our worries..
are the people who are our route,
are the folks who are our root
The one who is our way, is the
one who is in our happiest day

Assurance

Never commit on something not sure
Be sure of anything that's
thoroughly pure
There is hardly problem
that goes without cure
A woman must not be trusted,
if she pretends demur
Everything can be attracted,
one must know how to lure

Mother

She's my vision, she's my shoot
She's my way, she's my route
She makes my day, in
her lies my root
I'm her fertility, I'm her fruit
She can't be robbed off in loot
With her I stay forever,
in her reboot
For me, any distance
she can commute
She wipes away enemies who're brute
She is a melody, sweet
as tune of flute
She's a sweet person, she's very cute
She's a lady of high repute
She always prevents a case of dispute
A forthcoming danger,
she can compute
With her positivity, life
can never mute

She's my mother, humble
and without hoot
A lady of vigour, challenging
in her pursuit
Passionate human; juggling and jute

Advice

To understand my "Little Tanie" series better, I'd advise my readers to develop an admiration for the four songs I completely adore; they are "Connected", "Two Voices, One Song" and "We're Gonna Find It" from the movie, Barbie and The Diamond Castle; and the song, "This Is Me" from the motion picture The Barbie Diaries.

These, including the movie Barbie in a Christmas Carol have influenced and inspired me to become the person I am today and produce my "Little Tanie" books.

Movie Now and Then has greatly nurtured the artist in me; something that could motivate me to come up with some delicate ideas, bringing about the nourishment which an eager audience seeks.

Other than these, I have written over thousands of poems, some are in Hindi. They rest in decorative scrap books which are with my Godfather "Guru ji". In order to explore those treasures, you can come to his home:

Vindhyavaasini
(Behind Maarwaari Hospital)
Bara Dev
Godowlia
Varanasi
U.P.
India